Monde Merveillux!

Adult Coloring Book

AWESOME ANIMALS

Hand-drawn illustrations by Rene Rodis

ISBN-10:1535146222
ISBN-13: 978-1535146227

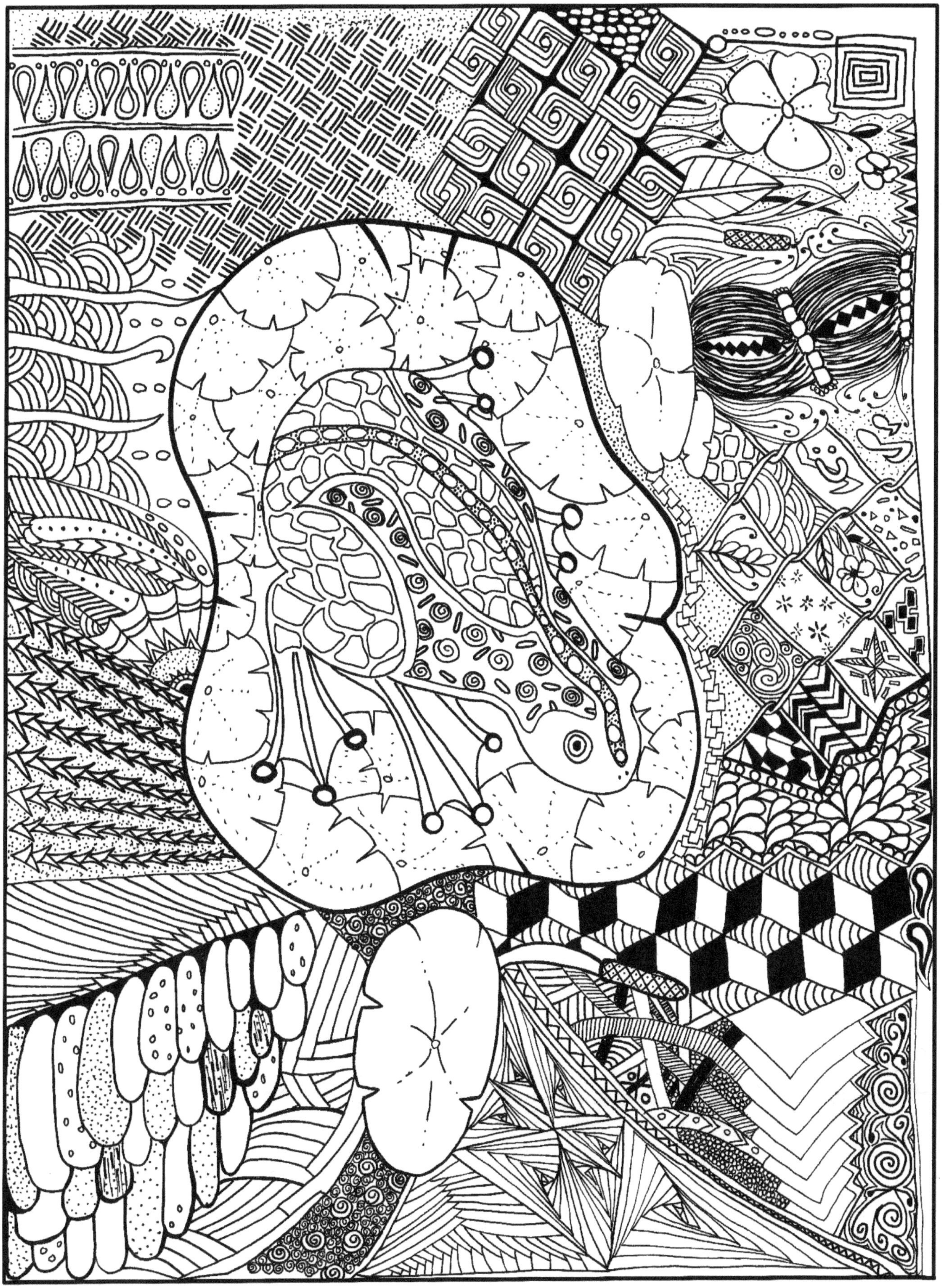

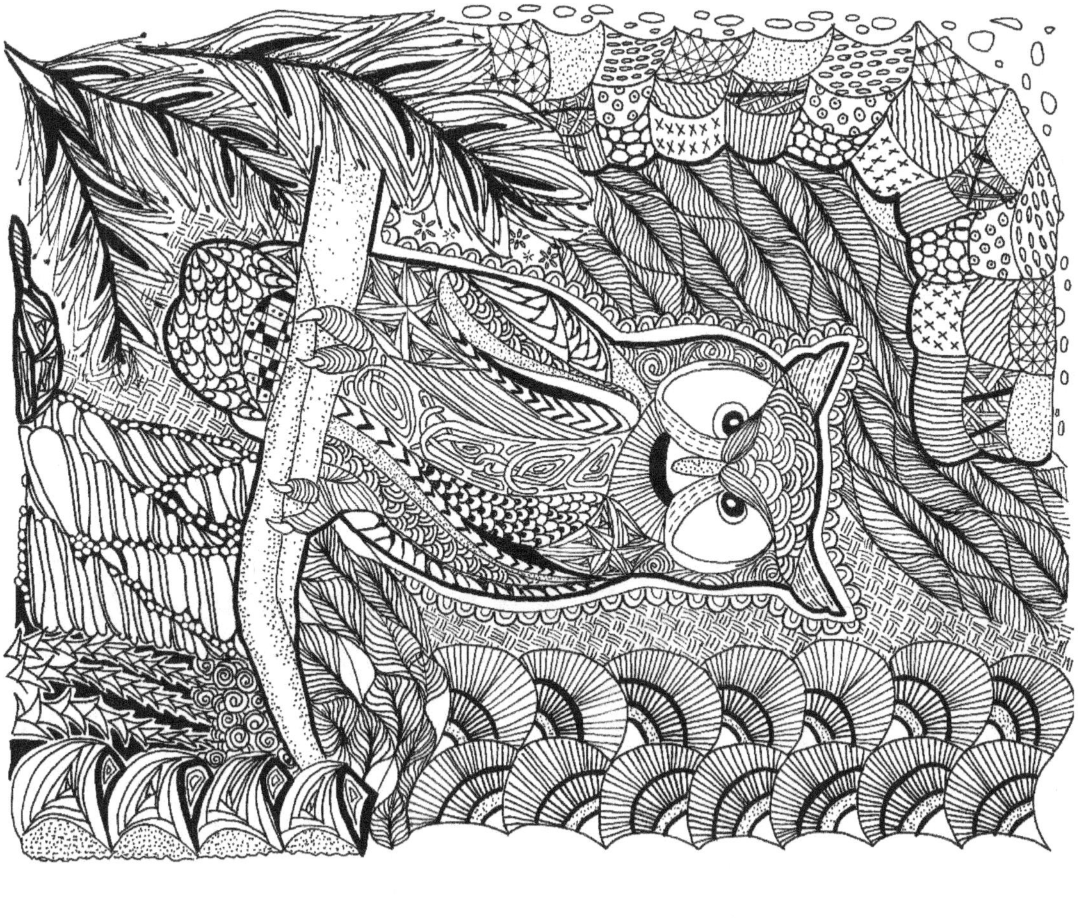

www.ingramcontent.com/pod-product-compliance
Lightning Source LLC
Chambersburg PA
CBHW081121280526
45787CB00007B/2923
9781535146227